All of You Is Welcome Here

Copyright © Rami 2022

All rights reserved. No part of this book may be reproduced or used in any manner without written permission of the copyright owner except for the use of quotations in a book review.

First paperback edition March 2022

Illustrated by Dana Bucur
Book design by Publishing Push

Print ISBN : 978-1-80227-324-3
eBook ISBN : 978-1-80227-325-0

@mymumpoet

All of You Is Welcome Here
A Self-Love Poetry Book

by
Rami

A Self-Love Poetry Book

Mama's Thoughts...

For anyone who needs something to hold on to—these poems provide understanding, acceptance, **self-belief, gentle encouragement, and hope**.

A place where you can feel truly at ease, embraced and cocooned with self-love. Read each poem daily for inspiration, or all in one but I would like this book to be your very own Home from Home.

Please cosy up with a warm drink, a fluffy blanket, sit with nature or whatever your comforts may be, turn the pages and have some time for yourself.

My Story...

I first started writing because I wanted to give my son a poem to thank him for a lovely Mother's Day. I wanted to have something that reminded him of our relationship. From this, I noticed I could not stop writing poems, and I was drawn to topics of self-love and words of encouragement to help people to feel better. Poetry itself also became the nurturing space that I needed as a mother.

I merely want to provide a safe and judgement-free environment for anyone to reflect, feel understood and accepted by all their emotions. Hopefully, I can help provide you with the courage to express yourself as well. I aspire to be a friend that you can confide in and be your true self with.

Ultimately, I want to provide and help to encourage a positive difference to people's mental health through the medium of poetry.

This is for my son, who directed me to this journey.

Please see the *first-ever* poem I ever wrote, just for you:

Viran's Mum:
Being your Mother is like Heaven on Earth; I know you like your planets, so they are in each verse.
You saved my life, brightened with warmth and love, something only Venus is capable of.
With your infectious smile and indomitable will, I can see Saturn being proud of your skill.
To be happy and strong, and always feel like you belong, is what my dreams are for you as your Mother.
When I am with you, I feel the Sun; Mercury is the closest, so I'm just like that one.
You have the biggest heart, Jupiter is envious, but never competes, nor makes it obvious.
For your humility is what will get you through; the Universe will always be there for you.
Lastly, when you're feeling blue, Neptune will speak and say, "Mummy is with you all the way".
Let us look together; I am sure we can see Mars, we will have a little dance under the stars…

Thank you for making me your mummy. Today, on Mother's Day and every day… I love you to the moon and back. You are my planets, stars and solar system. My whole Universe. Love from My Mum (As you call me) xx

A Poem about Self-Love

Magic in a bottle,
Pearls and Diamonds,
Anything that flickers,
Do not be frightened.

Drink the passion,
Drape your shoulders with magnificence,
Ignite your dreams,
Beauty is innocence.

Fresh ideas,
Creativity seeps through,
Change your narrative,
Let it work wonders for you.

Think in a new way,
Explore diverse realms,
With self-love, you will transform,
A ravishing butterfly effect,
Pure, wholly and divine.

Contents

I. Self-Belief	1	II. Gentle Encouragement	25
I Am a Butterfly	3	Paint Me a Picture	27
Solitude	4	Keep Going	28
Unconditional Love	5	Just Breathe	29
The Power of Praise	6	My Walks	30
Your Face	7	Letting Go	31
I See You	8	The 1st Step Is the Hardest	32
You're Better Than Me	9	Take Your Time	33
Someone Like Me	10	Try Again	34
Sweetheart	11	Find Your Feet	35
I Am Good Enough	12	Enough	36
You Amaze Me	13	Go with the Flow	37
Rose	14	Cool Waters	38
Doubt	15	Move Mountains	39
You Are Right	16	Vision Board	40
Trust Yourself	17	Hear My Voice	41
This Is for You	18	Reassurance	42
Push Yourself	19	Eyes	43
Add Value	20	Mirror	44
Purpose	21	Touch	45
Protect Your Energy	22	Picture Perfect	46
Believe in Your Magic	23	Heart 2 Heart	47

III. Hope — 49

One Day at a Time — 51
Everything will be Okay — 52
Tired — 53
Dreams — 54
Against All Odds — 55
Grief — 56
Faith — 57
Act of Kindness — 58
Spring — 59
Extraordinary — 60
Future Is Now — 61
No Matter What — 62
What Truly Matters — 63
Better Days — 64
Live and Let Live — 65
Be Kind — 66
Loyalty — 67
Glass Half Full — 68
Hold Your Head Up High — 69
Shine Bright — 70
New Beginnings — 71

IV. Welcome Home — 73

Go Inside — 75
Dig Deep — 76
Home Is What You Make It — 77
You Belong — 78
A Person of Few Words — 79
Open Your Door — 80
An Accepting Space — 81
Love Is a Journey — 82
My First Place — 83
The Moon — 84
Mother Nature — 85
The World — 86
Wanderlust — 87
Free Spirit — 88
Fly — 89
Sit with Yourself — 90
Your Truth — 91
Stay Safe — 92
Place Your Hand — 94
Home Comforts — 95
I See My Home in You — 98

Final Thoughts — 99

Stay Empowered — 99

A little bit about the author — 100

Acknowledgements — 101

A Forever Book for You (Viran) — 102

Chapter I.

Self-Belief

CHAPTER I. SELF-BELIEF

I Am a Butterfly

———

I have so much detail, the eye cannot see.
    Even if you look closely, you won't see all of me.
I am pretty, I am colourful, and I flutter happily.
    No one can catch me now; I have set myself free.
With endurance and delicate wings, I did always try.
    Something I am highly proud of, the fact that I can fly.
To people I remain a symbol of hope, I signify a beautiful form.
    I am here to remind you that through this you were born.
I am a butterfly; I am showing you that I am here.
    You can spread your wings now, and finally vanquish this fear!

———

Solitude

I am essential for your mental health and your well-being.
I have a quality of state that you are not really seeing.
Be alone for a minute, breathe in some power.
Let it build up until you pass the hour.
I am here to help you, to make you feel self-love.
I want to protect you like a hand feels within a glove.
Take your time to challenge the uncertainty within.
Let your calm nature and stability win.

Chapter I. Self-Belief

Unconditional Love

———

When you're accepted for every single flaw, you forget the pain of feeling raw.
You're vulnerable, but with someone there, it is safe for you to stop and to share.
A look in the eye, a hand held tight, is enough to tackle any fight.
 It is pure and so incredibly true; it will always be good to you.
Don't be scared though it does not leave, they love you for who you are;
 All you have to do is simply breathe.

———

The Power of Praise

It's so easy to covet, desire and praise other people,
Taking merely a second, to forget the importance of our own delight.
It is so hard to praise ourselves, especially when we're all alone at night.
It lasts a lifetime, so this we must do,
To say wonderful words and let them take care of you.
Praise yourself as much as you praise others, stand just as tall.
Fill your heart with gratitude and watch the doubts surrounding you fall.

CHAPTER I. SELF-BELIEF

Your Face

―――――

I can't look into your eyes; you make me feel nervous.
    I try to look, but quickly I swerve.
Your face is dazzling, just like a star in the sky.
    I will never see anything more beautiful, even if I try.
Contour and highlight are products you don't need.
    Your striking features clearly take the lead.
Please don't turn your face away, I will eventually look.
    But let me catch my breath first, the one that you just took.

―――――

I See You

I see the sleepless nights, your eyes look so tired.
I see the hunger in your belly, and how you are inspired.
I see the anxiety and the worry, your head seems to pound.
I see the love in your heart, and all the joy that you have found.
I see the quietness in your voice, your insecurities are heightened.
I see the confidence in your presence, despite you being frightened.
I see your mixed emotions, they go either way.
I see every single part of you, remember, it is okay not to be okay.

Chapter I. Self-Belief

You're Better Than Me

———

I have found myself saying this most of the time,
    To people I have only met, they always seem to be so fine.
I wonder what it is like to be them, so confident and sure,
    Do they ever look at me and feel this insecure?
In their presence, my stomach will turn,
    I wonder if this is something which I can unlearn.
I want to be able to put more than a few words together,
    To feel light around them just like a feather.
We are all the same, with self-love I will see,
    It takes time to be comfortable with just being me.

———

Someone Like Me

I used to put everyone on a pedestal,
It was always me, not them, taking the hardest fall.
I saw myself as last, you as number one,
My people-pleasing skills were second to none.
It has taken so much pain and patience to understand my worth,
But with love, this has been embraced.
Finally, someone like me I value,
I am deserving of being first-placed.

CHAPTER I. SELF-BELIEF

Sweetheart

———

She is deserving of a love, so eternal and true,
  Look around, you will see her standing next to you.
She is the girl next door, the one whose smile stops your track,
  She is the one who has everything that most people lack.
She is everybody's friend, available at every hour,
  She is the one that no one wants when everything turns sour.
She sings and even dances, to her it is not enough,
  Her talents are what makes her, but it is hard to always feel so tough.
She is a sweetheart, who treats people so well,
  One day her time will come and she will forget she ever fell.

———

I Am Good Enough

Waves hit me,
Sunken.
I need some relief,
It feels deep-rooted,
But this is just a floating belief.
It will take some time, and of course persistence and skill,
I am good enough; nothing will ever be as strong as my will.
Nurturing myself once again,
Go back to the beginning, stay there for a while, persevere with self-love,
You will get there in the end.

CHAPTER I. SELF-BELIEF

You Amaze Me

You sing, you dance, you cook, you draw, your work is spectacular,
Everything you touch turns to gold, it seems to be in your nature.
You work so hard to perfect your art, yet it does not seem to faze you,
I wish I could understand how you do all of this just by looking at you.
People admire how you express yourself; they just want to be your friend,
You amaze me every single day, don't forget your drive, true passions never end.

Rose

How can something so
graceful experience so much
pain?
Thorns stab my side.

How can something so
settled go through it all
again?
Hurt ruptures my veins.

How can something so
fragile find the strength to
remain?
Power dilutes my nerves.

I am still,
I am silent,
I am strong,
And I blossom, to break free of
this chain.

Chapter I. Self-Belief

Doubt

One of the strongest thoughts in our mind,
    Is of doubt, it constantly plays on rewind.
Even when it seems to disappear,
    It creeps in to instill more fear.
You wonder if its strength will last forever,
    Or just a season like bad weather.
I know the problem is pointing to you,
    It seems that doubt is a gentle cue.
Self-doubt is reminding us to go within,
    To go forward with self-love, and press play to win.

You Are Right

Somehow you just know,
Familiar like the sound of your mother's voice,
To do the right thing,
More than a guide,
A flame that will never hide.

Scarlet eyes,
Blazing fever in your heart,
It will keep coming,
Sometimes it will break you,
A wildfire of truth knocking to come in,
To remind you,
You are right.

Clasp this bonfire of courage,
Burn the pain,
That you were ever wrong,
Never, ever doubt your spirit again.

CHAPTER I. SELF-BELIEF

Trust Yourself

―――――

Words leave their mouth,
Spearmint cool,
Frozen from lies,
A lack of direction,
Chilled, white eyes.

Surface cracks,
Self-love triumphs,
Melt the ice,
Trust yourself first,
Don't think twice.

―――――

This Is for You

You may not even understand,
Hesitant to welcome my words,
This is for you though, to say that with you I stand.
In the midst of the haze and the frequent blurry days,
I see how much you tried,
I feel when you are afraid and why you want to run away and hide.
Fear does settle,
Slowly but surely,
Sprinkle self-care,
Build on your worth,
You are not alone,
Not while I am with you on this Earth.

Chapter I. Self-Belief

Push Yourself

A lionheart,
Roar sounds,
Never be afraid to go out of bounds.

Spill colour over the lines,
Smash the paintbrush,
Never settle until you feel that rush.

Imagination conquers reality,
Unleash a miracle,
Push yourself,
Achieve the unimaginable.

ALL OF YOU IS WELCOME HERE

Add Value

Whispering voices,
You'll matter as long as you're useful,
You'll be valued for the length your beauty lasts.
Worries that clip our wings,
Questions carry heavyweight,
Dimming views on what is real.

Write a love letter,
What if you believe that you can?
What if you decide to love yourself?
Echoes so profound,
Elegant words of value,
Endearing truth and sounds.

Embrace yourself fully,
I love myself unconditionally,
Add value to yourself,
With admiration and grace,
Positive droplets,
A smile beams from my face.

CHAPTER I. SELF-BELIEF

Purpose

You make the world a better place.
When your voice is silent,
Whisper tenacity,
It is not a race.

You excite someone out there.
Take your first step,
React inspiringly,
It is your momentum.

You will get there in time;
One day you will see,
Project confidence,
That is the finishing line.

Protect Your Energy

Disconnected from people,
Conversations you did not hear,
Better for you,
Bruised ear.

Removed from places,
Flourishing into space,
Serving you,
Glowing face.

Something bigger is protecting you,
Driven by love,
Don't give up now,
Guided from above.

CHAPTER I. SELF-BELIEF

Believe in Your Magic

───────

There is one important thing that I want to give to you—
Encouragement.
Kick down the barriers!
See what I see, clear of all the tears.
You have to believe in your magic,
Dreams do manifest.
Once you have a taste of this,
In yourself, you will always invest!

───────

Chapter II.
Gentle Encouragement

Chapter II. Gentle Encouragement

Paint Me a Picture

Paint me a picture, show me what I should see,
Keep going, so you bring your life to me.
Paint me a picture, show me each and every detail,
Keep going, so into your mind I can sail.
Paint me a picture, so I can step into your shoes,
Never stop, understanding is what I seek to find and never lose.

Keep Going

Don't underestimate the impact of your presence, you have such a gift,
Don't stop what you are doing, even if it feels like you can't keep going.
Don't put yourself down, your character is already so humble,
Don't question yourself, or your ability, the answers are all within you.
Keep going,
The only way out is through,
I am holding your hand as your doubts hurt me too.
Keep going,
Push clear of this last obstacle,
Break down all barriers, remember that anything is possible.

Chapter II. Gentle Encouragement

Just Breathe

———

Breathe.
If you feel any panic,
Just Breathe.
Remember your strong will.
Breathe.
If you feel betrayed,
Just Breathe.
Start to finally heal.
Breathe.
If you are hurt from yesterday,
Just Breathe.
Don't be ruled by the past,
Breathe.
If the future scares you,
Just Breathe.
Don't run ahead so fast.
Breathe.
Focus on the present day,
Just Breathe.
You have got this; I am with you all the way.

———

My Walks

Ready to walk, I charge my phone,
    Secretly in fear of being alone.
Worried I have nowhere to go, I step outside the door,
    Immediately I know that I want more.
Inside, I feel comfort and affection,
    Pleased with myself that I took this direction.
Pulled by the wind, I surrender,
    The silence around me feels ever so tender.
I may be alone, but I am never lonely,
    I have a breath of fresh air that is finally beside me.

CHAPTER II. GENTLE ENCOURAGEMENT

Letting Go

―――――

Burdened thoughts,
Propped with weighted shoulders,
Heavy heart,
Possessed with resistance.

Intertwining words,
Expressed with difficulty,
Turbulent emotions,
Trapped with no rescue.

Why do we talk down to ourselves?
Forgetting that we have been burnt.
Why do we not pause and breathe?
Lessons take time to be learnt.

With each pulse I let go,
Each idea moves me closer,
To the space I desire,
One day this will all be over.

―――――

The 1st Step Is the Hardest

Running shoes and a stopwatch,
Steamy perspiration.
Yearning for the finish line,
Gives me my inspiration.
Succeeding my personal best.

Upward hills and soaking up the views,
Blisters and muscle gain.
Every time you feel like giving up,
Fuel your drive again.
Aspiring to work hard.

The first step is the hardest,
It is also the one you did overcome,
It was where you first started,
Look how far you have come.

Chapter II. Gentle Encouragement

Take Your Time

―――――――

When people tell me all of their fears, I pray for an end to their falling tears.
You don't have to have all of the answers, alleviate the pressure and expectation,
You will sometimes get things wrong, finding yourself in the wrong direction.
It is never too late to follow your heart, it doesn't matter if you didn't do it from the start.
One day at a time or step by step, whichever way you feel,
    Just take your time and let your purpose on this Earth be revealed.

―――――――

Try Again

Something that I've always tried to teach my little boy:
Is if at first you don't succeed,
You get up, try again and before you know it, you are in the lead.
It can be as simple as going down the slide,
It can be scary at first, but soon you enjoy the ride.
The cuts and bruises tell a story,
That getting back up will give you all the glory.
A sense of achievement, to build your self-esteem,
To dare is to do, go on, look ahead, and fulfil your dream.

Chapter II. Gentle Encouragement

Find Your Feet

A lifetime can be spent of trying to fit in,
Reassurance we naturally seek.
Not being invited makes us feel incredibly weak.
You wonder why it feels so cold.
To keep warm, we have to follow our own path,
Welcome the individual blessings.
Find your feet and realise that nothing was ever missing.

Enough

Questioning yourself should come with a score.
Ratings are high, but it won't stop you from asking for more.
Am I enough? Will it all last?
Everything multiplies;
A time will come when you will no longer need the whys.
Look into your core, take out all of the rubble,
Focus on the gold, unearth your potential.
Stay in your own lane,
The answers are within you, you will find them again and again.

Chapter II. Gentle Encouragement

Go with the Flow

———

Nobody wants the worry of tomorrow, to feel the weight on one's shoulder.
How do we seek reassurance that the next day will be brighter?
Just like the river, the waves can hit a rock,
Finding its balance immediately, once it has passed its shock.
Start slowly, take it easy and go with the flow.
Your core will be hit with emotion now and then, but your world will quickly adapt.
The rock is like your core, strong and able to deflect any pain,
Inside you are tender, remember this, and your peace will always remain.

———

Cool Waters

Dive in,
Locate your pulsating pain,
Bubbling underground.

Deep breath,
Self-talk, it's ok,
Rise to the surface.

Consistent practice,
Refreshing support bands,
Float all the way through.

Chapter II. Gentle Encouragement

Move Mountains

―――――――

My mother used to always say that she raised me with her two hands,
Since I have become a mum myself, that is my ambition too.
You never realise the miracles your hands are;
They feed, wipe away your tears, and provide that gentle touch.
Please look after them as they really don't want much.
If they can raise a life, and help you stay alive,
They look fragile, but trust me, they know how to survive.
So go on, believe in your hands, and use them with all of your might,
Move mountains, I promise you will get the best view in sight.

―――――――

Vision Board

A floating hand,
A limitless pen,
That is how I will guide you.

A distinctive affirmation,
An articulate statement,
That is how I will remember you.

A hush to the surrounding noise,
A quiet shift,
That is how I will centre you.

A daily execution,
A trust in your mark,
That is how I will change you.

Chapter II. Gentle Encouragement

Hear My Voice

———

Never have I been more vulnerable,
Standing here looking over crowds,
Seas, rivers of people,
I have a soreness in my heart, it aches.

Deep breaths I have spoken,
It shakes, but it is mine,
My voice out of this cage,
Feel my intention.

No one has what I have,
Weakness has vanished,
Bravery has wrapped itself around,
Speak your truth, even if you cannot hear,
We can all see you, and not this fear.

———

Reassurance

Self-talk so fearless,
Honest feedback imprints,
Soul, I will remind you.

Consistent in approach,
Tall, balanced spine,
Body, I will steady you.

Countless years of inner work,
Quietly confident nearby,
Mind, I will enable you.

Soft-hearted persona,
Secure attachment deepens,
Heart, I will stick by you.

Trust its process,
Exchange connections,
Spirit, I will look after you.

Chapter II. Gentle Encouragement

Eyes

Silver lines,
Hidden in the creases.
Freckles popping,
Bridge of the nose.

Shiny pearls,
Perfect vision.
Glossy lashes,
Full of life.

Milky white,
Deep blue sea.
Precision eyeliner,
Angled each corner.

Contrast in time,
Old and new.
Decorated beautifully,
Colours stay alive.

Mirror

When someone projects their insecurities onto us, they get heightened.
When we look in the mirror, we appear frightened.
Assuming the worst, if only we could recognise the good in others,
And handle each trait with respect.
Ourselves too, let us not reject.
Your intuition tells us to accept,
Visualise positivity, radiate love and good energy,
The touchstone of virtue.
To live with yourself is to live with this sincerity.

CHAPTER II. GENTLE ENCOURAGEMENT

Touch

Only you and I know,
This sensation.
It binds us together,
Sparks that jump,
But always connect.
To provide comfort,
And create meaning,
There is simply no better feeling.
Seek this whenever you can,
Reach out.
Live wire electricity,
From the pit of your stomach.
A beautiful presence is there,
To say that I will carry you,
And I will always care.

Picture Perfect

I wonder how many of us feel the need to post only highlights to our feed?
It's obvious we're all hiding behind a caption, hashtags to say that we are having fun.
Deep down, we really want others to see that I am like you and you are like me.
We crave a connection, now even more so, we wish everything was not just for show.
It takes time to show that authenticity is better, nothing beats writing a simple honest letter.
Let us address real life and show,
    That it is a rejoiceful experience, more than we know!

Chapter II. Gentle Encouragement

Heart 2 Heart

———

The power of a simple conversation—
The impact is unreal,
It is a wondrous medicine,
For heartbreaks to finally heal.
Opening up to someone is like hearing your heart's rhythm,
Amplified beats,
Crashing waves,
The base pounds,
Souls are in each other's hands.
Believe in your gut and what you are receiving,
It is part of the plan,
Listen to the trust, it wants your attention.
Your hearts have finally met,
No one can take this away from you,
Real connections never forget.

———

CHAPTER III.

Hope

Chapter III. Hope

One Day at a Time

I have often found myself living for tomorrow,
    Getting lost in thought and predicting every sorrow.
In the past, I catch myself too,
    Looking over my shoulder, it is not the best view.
The present is the place I feel the most serene,
    It deserves all my attention and needs to be seen.
Time is not something to sacrifice,
    Take one day at a time and follow this advice.

Everything will be Okay

Not everything will go the way we once planned,
Secure to lose everything at the drop of a hand.
People will raise you up, but they will also let you down,
You can struggle forever, or just see the larger plan.
Whether you go left or right, follow your instinct's guiding light,
The secret is in trusting yourself, believing that everything will be okay.
Have strength for a little bit longer,
Go get that better day.

CHAPTER III. HOPE

Tired

I am Tired,
Every day is not fine.
I am Tired,
All I want is some time.
I am Tired,
Forever in a haze.
I am Tired,
Finding no way through this maze.
I am Tired,
My eyes are heavy.
I am Tired,
Forever walking steady.
I am Tired,
Trying to have a rest.
I am Tired,
Of taking this test.
I am Tired,
Of feeling nothing.
I am Tired,
Of never being something.
Look after me now for when I am sleeping,
I will need your strength to stop me from weeping.
My rested eyes will one day awake, my life will take that good turn,
This candle inside will no longer need to burn.

Dreams

Dreams, my happy place,
Crash into the pillow, silk satin sheet.
My body slumps but lifts my feet,
Up, up into the air I go,
Wrapped in a cotton cloud, just like my fluffy bed socks.
I escape for a moment, this mind unlocks,
Emotions swim to the surface,
Raw but I am starting to heal,
I wake up in the morning remembering how to feel.
Embrace the stillness,
Let go, you don't have to try,
You got through the day, now you are free to fly.

CHAPTER III. HOPE

Against All Odds

You will reach your goals even if the world seems against you,
People will look down to point out every single flaw,
But the wind will hit their judging face.

Dusty eyes—

You blinded them, they are secretly in awe,
Scare them with your determination,
Let them whisper, your intensity will build,
No one will move you now, you are protected,
Wrapped by this perfect diamond shield.

Grief

Agony is so difficult, words cannot describe,
    Day after day we try to survive.
All experiences are different, but so deeply raw,
    It seems we are all fighting the exact same war.
We struggle to talk, to say we cannot cope,
    Clinging on to messages of comfort and hope.
A majestic feather falls softly by our side,
    We want that spirit to be our guide.
Following the signs, it seems only true,
    No one goes forever, they just look after you.

CHAPTER III. HOPE

Faith

Blindsided by injury,
A kick to the stomach.
Chicken soup for the soul,
Faith is my cure.

Running out of steam,
About to throw the towel in,
A turn of events,
Faith is my strength.

Gloves are my second skin,
Knuckles are black and blue.
Alarm bells will ring,
Faith is my protection.

Act of Kindness

I will never forget a certain time in my past,
    Where I sat on a bench, wondering how long
    this sadness would last.
Along came a woman, who sat down next to me,
    She talked all about her troubles with her family.
I listened as she sought my attention,
    She trusted me without any question.
She made me feel that my opinion mattered,
    I urged her to listen to her heart, despite it being shattered.
We talked about what she should do,
    It seemed that she needed a safe place too.
It made me forget about all of my pain,
    I noticed I spread joy and I yearned to do it again.
Do not underestimate a single act of kindness, no matter how
    big or small,
It can change someone's life and encourage them not to fall.

CHAPTER III. HOPE

Spring

This for me is the best time of year,
It is a fresh beginning where all becomes clear.
Daffodils open, and trees blossom too,
A pale pink colour, the world appears brand new.
Old habits and thoughts are things of the past,
A new season is upon us, long may it last.
I love the glistening river and the warm sun on my face,
I feel I have more energy for the dreams I'm about to chase.
My birthday falls on the fifth of May, I wish for more light,
Everyone can now see that there is an end in sight.

Extraordinary

We show the highs that we think define us,
The lights, the glitz and the glamour.
A rush that is always short-lived,
Look to value the simple things in life.
Country parks, woods and coastal cliffs,
Birds serenading, the sweet smell of candy floss.
Giggling children, a high that is more precious than most,
I was taught to magnify the extraordinary in the ordinary.
It will give you the most divine fulfilment,
I owe my life and being to this person.

Their words are the secret to contentment.

CHAPTER III. HOPE

Future Is Now

It is hard to live in the present,
When the future is so uncertain.
Looking ahead without control,
I am sure it is not just me feeling this way.
We are all taking it day by day,
The future is now, it seems.
Each moment is how we have to play it,
Whatever hurts you, let it go, it is now or never.
Don't dull this moment with distractions,
Please don't ruin your forever.

No Matter What

I am always searching and seeking solace in every breath,
Someone or something to be there no matter what.
The difference between my possessions and desires is drastic,
I tend to yearn for a safe space all the time.
My right hand is out, reaching to soothe your raging storm,
My heart is open, wanting to keep you emotionally warm.
Look within, hold your hand and trust your heart,
I am your hope and comfort too, please don't pull me apart.

Chapter III. Hope

What Truly Matters

―――――

The smallest of walls can hold the greatest of laughs,
Warmth, comfort, the occasional tear.
Mainly happy ones of minute wins and exciting news,
With the odd cry about the things that we lose.
It is inevitable in life to have both ups and downs,
You don't have to have the best to have a good round.
Where you feel at home is what truly matters,
A person, a place, the walks or whatever you please,
An aroma of spices, the sip of your morning tea.
Cinnamon bagels, eggs and the delight of fresh coffee,
Sensations and tastes that can't be replaced.
A pull so strong, it will always take you to a place,
Where you will feel the most at ease and live with serenity and grace.

―――――

Better Days

Tedious twenty-four hours,
A dull, constant pace.
Why do we always think the worst?
Better Days are already here,
There is nothing left to chase.

Colourful, satin material,
A tapestry of delight.
Our presence is meticulously wrapped.
Better Days are already here,
We have a gift to see the world,
Faith and sight.

CHAPTER III. HOPE

Live and Let Live

Expectations that destroy,
First scar on bare skin,
Breathe out the ego.

Take a step back,
Blend into the background,
Do your own thing.

Focus on your passion,
Design is lonely,
Worth every second.

Close this chapter,
Last message to convey,
Live and Let Live.

A small price to pay,
For peace and better days.

Be Kind

Feet on the ground,
Soiled toes.
Hands toward the rain,
Drenched fingers.

Tread carefully,
Earth is precious.
Quick embrace,
Sky is charming.

Inflict no pain,
Enchanted being.
Absorb only good,
Valuable treasure.

CHAPTER III. HOPE

Loyalty

A whirlwind in the chest,
Lifted heart.
A settled stomach,
Untangled gut.

A forever smile,
Clear mind.
A joyous laugh,
Untied tongue.

A lifelong tonic,
Best friend.
A wellbeing inside,
Flawless loyalty.

Glass Half Full

Bottled feelings,
Shattered into tiny pieces,
Blood-stained hands.

Open up,
Some people misunderstand,
Sour bitter taste.

Time passes,
Freedom trickles through,
Bright shining reflection.

Aromas linger,
Wrapped mature flavours,
Sipping sweet victory.

CHAPTER III. HOPE

Hold Your Head Up High

―――――

Why do we always look to the ground?
Look up!
I would rather stare at the cobbles,
Than have your eyes pierce through me,
Your judgment burns inside my soul.
Look up!
Avoid the gaze.
Do what is necessary,
It is ok to look after yourself.
Look up!
Hold your head up high,
That is your guide,
No one else,
But that pure blue sky.

―――――

Shine Bright

Magnetic is your personality,
Heroic in your stance,
You have touched many lives,
And saved more than you know.
You sense a grey cloud,
Thunder and storm,
Don't let anyone cloud your sparkle,
Keep yourself warm.
Notice the rays behind you,
Sunshine and stars,
Shine bright,
I have your back,
Even in the dark night.

Chapter III. Hope

New Beginnings

Why do we always look to the future?
Frozen with fear,
Replace with hope,
To enter each year.
Our minds replay negative thoughts,
Forgetting all the battles that we have fought.
We don't have to suffer love,
Let us live like butterflies,
With sunshine, freedom and a little flower pulled apart.
But with faith, we have grown into,
A most magnificent piece of art.

CHAPTER IV.

Welcome Home

CHAPTER IV. WELCOME HOME

Go Inside

If only we knew this right from the start,
That we have to love ourselves first,
Tolerating less and less,
Hearts would never fall apart.
Establish boundaries and call it self-love,
Home is within,
Climb the walls,
For foundations to be lifted.
Drench your roots with love,
And let it seep into your essence,
Feed with organic seeds,
To filter each vessel.
A wholesome heart,
Blood is pumping,
Take care of your insides,
Live long and honour thy name.

Dig Deep

How can you plant your own roots,
In a culture so narrow water cannot retain?
Dig deep,
Replenish yourself again.

Use all of your tools,
Expand to the wider community,
Look, Learn and Listen,
Every presence lasts an eternity.

Interpret your own world,
You can rebirth,
Nourish your forever home,
Our Beloved Earth.

Build on your worth,
Riches and soil,
Watch yourself flourish,
Conscious and Loyal.

CHAPTER IV. WELCOME HOME

Home Is What You Make It

———————

My mother always says:
Your attitude determines your outcome;
She says this with passion and a smile.
Each day is an opportunity to paint your home new,
Decorate it with joy and spring-clean it too.
Luck comes when you least expect it,
You don't have to carry the past,
Polish the shelves, look after them so they last.
Wherever you live, wherever it is, make it a home,
And all of this will set the tone.

———————

You Belong

It doesn't matter who you are,
Or how much you have,
Relationships in between,
Broken,
Through no fault of your own.
The universe is there,
Holding a hand,
Lovingly on your right shoulder,
You belong,
Rest your feet,
Road to road,
House to house,
Person to person,
Wherever you go.
You are a part of everything you brush,
It comes to life,
Delicate,
Like the essence of who you are.

Chapter IV. Welcome Home

A Person of Few Words

People always joke and wonder,
You say a few words, but what is all of that under?
Is it knowing confidence, to speak and blow us all away?
Or is it a shyness that is always here to stay?
To speak not so often is mysterious indeed.
Behind all of us though, everyone's voice has a need.
The concentrated gazes, and wait for every word, is that the intention?
To have everyone guessing, what are they about to mention?
See, we never really know anyone, not even the ones who shout.
What we need to do is stop ourselves and ask, what is it all about?
Words, voices, speaking and silence, they all can be so very few,
Be kind and welcome them home.
We never really know the colour of someone's feelings, or if they are blue.

Open Your Door

All homes carry a story,
Families intertwined,
Generations separated,
Memories within the walls,
Conversations overheard,
You never really know what goes on behind closed doors.
No one has the right to judge a place,
That they have never lived in,
Walk in their shoes,
You don't know unless you're in that situation,
No soul knows what options they had to choose.
You can make a positive difference though,
Open your door and be kind,
Be that home to someone,
The one that they are always trying to find.

Chapter IV. Welcome Home

An Accepting Space

———

Thrive, not survive,
Home's welcoming mantra,
A creative space,
Accepting of any face.

Pen to paper,
Positive words and affirmations,
Inspiring voices,
Safe to make our own choices.

Rockets launching,
POWs of explosion,
Home is where you will land,
Safe to say, I will hold your hand.

———

Love Is a Journey

A word so powerful, it has many things that it could mean,
    Holds so much force and power, yet it still cannot be seen.
This word is found hidden deep within the heart,
    Something that grows or is felt right from the start.
The stronger it is, the louder it attempts to scream,
    It also causes pain, festering around until it becomes your theme.

Love is truly magical, it can make you fly so high,
    But I have decided to write in such a way as I cannot lie.
It is a vast emotion, that strongly pulls you in ever so deep,
    It carries expectations, a part of you that you always wish to keep.

It can leave you feeling drained, asking what does it all mean?
    But I feel this is part of the journey; every emotion must be seen.
It brings up anger, guilt and the most terrifying: fear,
    These are just a few I know, that appear too near.
I feel love provides us with a lesson, one of which is to be kind,
    I know this can take some time to process, but it is one
    we all have to find.

Chapter IV. Welcome Home

My First Place

———

You were the first place I ever laid my head, the first hand I ever saw,
    The first touch I ever felt and the first smile I ever wore.
You fed, you clothed and held me tight,
    You cradled me; I was never out of your sight.
Others held me and said I was lovely,
    You could not help but look over with concern and worry.
You carried me in your arms even though your bones were sore,
    Your heart was aching but it did not stop you giving me more.
A mother's love is a powerhouse of emotion,
    A body of strength and essence of pure devotion.
A mother's love is a secure place, one which we call home,
    It is a safe space, the first one you ever owned.

———

The Moon

Like the sun, you are bound to me,
Who else looks for it in times of trouble?
You know my innermost secrets,
Your orbit penetrates my chest,
My X-Ray,
I know you want me,
My Home, My Universe—I promise you I will always stay.

CHAPTER IV. WELCOME HOME

Mother Nature

There are four seasons on this Earth,
Winter, autumn, summer and spring,
Just like us, they change—hibernating.
Temperamental,
Boiling inside,
Still and serene,
The water so calm,
Each one of them needs something.
Moods so different,
Supported by rivers, trees, sun and flowers,
Nature is their strength,
We can draw on this,
Muddy walks, singing in the rain,
The smell of freshly cut grass is back again.
Invigorating air, sunsets of burnt orange,
Self-love and letting others be,
Heal inside,
Grow at your own pace,
In Mother Nature, we have this space,
A home, where we can restore our being.

The World

Souls intertwined,
Ears pressed on smooth skin,
The world is silent.

Communication flows,
Spoken words of knowledge,
The world is full.

Senses heighten,
Surrounding sweet smells,
The world is captivating.

Focused lens,
A beauty in reflection,
The world is you.

CHAPTER IV. WELCOME HOME

Wanderlust

Turquoise skies and boarding gates,
Adventures at the airport.
Strangers talk, you feel their excitement,
A first dose of contentment.

Flip flops on the beach,
Lay down your hat.
Amongst the burning sand,
Your soulmate's hand.

Markets, textiles and wafting incense,
Seep into your pores.
Moonlight and candles,
Overlooking the distant shores.

Freshly caught fish,
Mouth watering homegrown tomatoes.
Soaking up cultures,
Taste the majestic ocean.

A strong desire for travel,
You must never ignore.
That is your home Wanderlust,
Explore more and more.

Free Spirit

It was you, when you were first born,
Before life made you frown.
It was you, when you left the world,
After the sun went down.

It was you, when you were alone,
Dancing in the moonlight.
It was you, in a crowded bar,
Ordering anything in sight.

It was you, when you were talking to strangers,
Anonymity was your thing.
It was you, acquainting your friends,
Social butterflies that sing.

It was you, it will always be you,
The person who treated everyone as their own.
It was you, and it will always be you,
You are everybody's home.

Chapter IV. Welcome Home

Fly

———

Perched on a rooftop,
Abundance of nutritious seeds,
Fueled to fly.

Wings now soaring,
Adrenaline kicks in,
Pledge to fly.

Soft landing to a different home,
Change is good,
Reason to fly.

Search for a meaning,
Delve into the unknown,
Commit to fly.

———

Sit with Yourself

What doesn't kill us, makes us stronger,
But in all seriousness, how do we heal from trauma?

Barbed wires, stinging nettles,
Caged within our minds, nothing settles.

Muscles tense, contracting spasm,
All that we fear, does not happen.

Clean intentions and an innocent face,
Crystal healing to clear the void and space.

Uncomfortable feelings,
Brittle, prickly sores.
Strengthened perseverance,
Polished in secret.

Close your eyes,
It is ok to be alone.
Sit with yourself,
Acceptance makes a home.

CHAPTER IV. WELCOME HOME

Your Truth

Unfamiliar surroundings, affectionate neighbours,
Lost and found.
Indestructible interior.

Doors slam, smiling reception,
Shut out or involved.
Looking within oneself.

Triggers and wounds,
Let nature take its course.
Healed and as one,
This is your Truth.

Stay Safe

Secure, loved, and never alone,
There are no cracks in your pure heart,
For danger to come in,
Suddenly, those flashbacks begin.

The rooms close in on you,
With your back against the wall,
You're unable to draw another breath,
Even your speech stalls.

Almond eyes don't feel so soft anymore,
They're stinging and sleepless with worry.
You've been made to feel unworthy,
"Why was I treated so badly?"

That is all you want to ask,
But they choose not to listen.

You have a jewel for a heart,
People feel this more than you know,
You can't help it if something doesn't feel right.

CHAPTER IV. WELCOME HOME

Alarmed with signs,
Tugs and resistance,
Inklings tear into you.

Red warnings—
Go into shelter;
That is your home.
Do whatever it takes!
It is okay,
To do what is right,
To stay safe,
To be in a place you don't have to fight.

———

Place Your Hand

Place a hand onto your forearm,
When the sun goes down and your shadow leaves you.

Place a hand onto your stomach,
When you rewrite history with flashbacks and clammy sweats.

Place a hand onto your heart,
When you discover a cold truth from hot lies.

Place a hand onto your side,
When the sharp words of others stab you profusely.

Place a hand onto your palm,
When you are desperate and need to extinguish the pain.

Place your hand into your own,
When you need to start again.

Hold yourself,
Rebuild if you have to,
You are home.

Chapter IV. Welcome Home

Home Comforts

Your throat is inflamed, drink some honey,
Wrinkled hands, hydrate them with cream,
Bones are crackling, a salt bath bomb,
Fizzy pop to the surface.
A massage for weighted shoulders,
Spray your perfume, create a scent,
Eyes are out of their sockets,
Circles and dark shadows,
Where have the days been spent?
Adrenaline rushing,
Sleep that extra hour,
Heart is heavy, mind in an overload.
Headphones, music and lost in walking,
Talk, talk and just keep on talking,
If you need five minutes—
Go hide in the toilet,
Put the kettle on, listen to that whistle,
Sip the hot tea; body feels sluggish,
Exercise, steam the room, and stretch ligaments,
Silver hairstreaks, it is all entangled,
You need tender loving care.

All of You Is Welcome Here

Thinking about others,
The grass is always greener,
Leave them be, nourish your own soil,
Talk to your people, the ones who lift you,
Friends, neighbours, or even strangers,
To connect like we used to,
Show off your smile, a hello over the fence,
Imperative to stay away from those,
Who wave flags which are red.
Stay close to people who nurture you instead,
Not those where you don't know where to tread.
Be careful, don't walk on glass,
Or eggshells as well,
Read and expand your mind,
Lead your own gentle path,
Your stomach is in knots again,
Boil some chicken broth,
Savour each steaming spoonful,
The taste of good health.

Life comes crumbling down:
Start again,
Home was not built in a day,
Like a jigsaw, the pieces just need to find their place.
Self-care is the glue,
Do not feel guilty for looking after you!
Respond to your needs,
As Maslow's hierarchy teaches,
We need to rest and recover,
You are good enough,
Once you know this,

Chapter IV. Welcome Home

Your mental health is what you will choose,
Prioritise this, no matter how much you regress.
Loving yourself is the lesson,
You have done it already; you have passed each test.
Being comfortable in your own skin,
Can fill your home even more,
This time it will last,
In touch with your inner core.

———

ALL OF YOU IS WELCOME HERE

I See My Home in You

I feel I have known you in a past lifetime,
    I have seen all your expressions before.
Your smile, the twinkle in your eye,
    I just want them more and more.
You are the roof over my head,
    I see my home in your face.
Home is a protected feeling,
    A calm and nurturing space.
Your arms carry my soul,
    Soothed by the warmth of your skin.
You have created a boundary,
    Not to let anyone bad in.
I don't want anything anymore,
    Just to be together.
I am blessed to reside in you,
    Forever and ever and ever.
Home equals pride,
    You have made this possible for me.
You have opened my heart,
    With your specially crafted key.
              I thank you for welcoming all of me.

Final Thoughts

Stay Empowered

Let the dust settle,
Days will pass,
Emotions watered down,
Rinsed of control.

In the midst of chaos,
Believe there is light,
Own your feelings,
You will sense it feels right.

Endurance to the rescue,
Bones warm from the heat,
Stepping back into self-love,
Remember, empowerment is ever so sweet.

A little bit about the author

Rami is an emerging poetess, author and proud mother whose lifelong vision is to encourage people to love themselves through heartfelt, poetic storytelling. Both compassionate and caring, she is also on a mission to provide a safe space for her readers to remind them that they are never truly alone on their journeys. No matter where someone resides on this beautiful and diverse planet, self-love is a healing force that brings about a positive change. When she isn't pouring her heart out onto paper, you can find this empathetic soul pampering herself, taking a relaxing bath, unwinding with a steaming cup of aromatic tea, exercising, or going on a healing nature walk.

Acknowledgements

Writing a poetry book has been effortless, enjoyable and more healing than I could have ever imagined. None of this would have been possible without my son, Viran. He has been my inspiration and has MADE me love myself. He has provided me with a whole new meaning of love.

I'm eternally grateful to my mum, who stood by me during my struggles. She taught me acceptance, generosity, manners, respect, and so much more that has helped me to feel fulfilled in life. I truly have no idea where I'd be if she had not supported me so selflessly.

To my dad, who is no longer on this Earth. He taught me to be hungry to learn, grow, and to be someone. He never stopped me; he only encouraged me. He was a man wiser than his years and a man who just accepted me for me. His gentle nature is very much in the words of my poems.

Although this period of my life was filled with many ups and downs, my coach and mentor, Riti Patel, kept me going and saved me when I needed it. She made me realise that this is my calling. She is one of a kind. People like this are angels sent to help you, so for that, I am extremely grateful.

To Dana, my illustrator: For sticking by me and allowing me to trust you with my vision. Your energy is a massive part of the book and this journey with me.

Thankful for a loving family and for the many friends I have made who have shown me encouragement, and kindness when I have really needed it. This is so rare to find, but something I hope lives on.

A Forever Book for You (Viran)

Hold the front cover, really tight,
Your little fingers will turn every page,
A bedtime story, looking through that telescope to the starry night.
The world is your oyster,
Scribble notes in the margins,
For you to explore.
Breathtaking landmarks in sight,
A journey to learn,
In your backpack and on every flight.
Make that positive difference,
Bookmarks and folded sheets,
I pray for you that everything will be alright.
Solace and comfort,
Near your bedside lamp,
Each chapter has a light.
Expressions in your tone,
All verses have my heart.
A story to tell a family of your own,
So we are never apart.
Learn from my experience,
Memorise the titles,
Self-love will keep you saved.
Embody every paragraph,
Instill each sentence,
These genuine intentions will never fade.

www.ingramcontent.com/pod-product-compliance
Lightning Source LLC
Chambersburg PA
CBHW020911080526
44589CB00011B/551